I Like to Play

written by Anne Giulieri

illustrated by Cherie Zamazing

I like to play in my yard.

I like to play at school, too.

I like to play on the big rocks in my yard.

At school I can play on the rock wall, too!

I like to play on the big hill in my yard.
I can go down the big hill.

At school I can go
down the slide, too!

I like to hide in the tree
in my yard.

At school I can hide
in the tunnel, too!

I like to play on the little log in my yard.

I can jump on the little log.

At school I can jump
on the big log, too!

15

Can you play in a yard?

Can you play at school, too?